THE MIDDLE PASSAGE:
105 DAYS

Estella Conwill Majozo

Africa World Press, Inc.

P.O. Box 1892   P.O. Box 48

Trenton, NJ 08607   Asmara, ERITREA

Africa World Press, Inc.

P.O. Box 1892      P.O. Box 48
Trenton, NJ 08607   Asmara, ERITREA

Cover Design: Ashraful Haque
Cover Artwork and Illustrations by Robert Douglas, Jr.

Catalog-in-Publication Data available from Library of Congress

ISBN 0-86543-981-8 (Hard cover)
ISBN 0-86543-982-6 (Paperback)

Dedication

to the 60 million and more
whose muted voices still await a full hearing

in memory of
Alex Haley, griot
Margaret Walker Alexander, poet
Dr. Darwin T. Turner, beloved teacher

A special thanks to

John Reed
Alva Hoskins
Doris Wooten
George Faison
Amelia Blossom Pegram
Woodie King
Houston Conwill
Dominic Alexander
            for listening

Patrice Sales Lowe
William Conwill
Anthonia Kalu
Papa Aly Ndaw
Capri Hawkins
Ingrid Reneau
Judylyn Ryan
Shauna Taylor
            for lending their voices
            to the sounding

"Middle Passage:
        voyage through death
            to life upon these shores"

                    Robert Hayden

and after fifty years
she hasn't forgotten
hasn't forgotten
how she had lain there
in her own blood
lain there in her own shit

bleeding memories in the darkness

                    Grace Nichols

1

I am Ramatoulaye!
Queen Ramatoulaye!
Even on this slave ship!
Even amidst these toubob beasts,
these white men
who beat us,
break our bones,
who try to banish our spirits
to the bottom of holding caves!
to the isolation of abandoned castles
that reek now of vomit and blood and foulest evil
which I refuse to submit to,
or allow the people
whom I love and lead to submit to either!
regardless of these wretched leg irons
or however many slave bans they cuff
across my resistance,
I am Queen Ramatoulaye
and I will deliver my people!

And I will also remember this!
Every part of this!
in honor of my husband, Mawdo,
    The Creator rest his soul—
who was murdered in defense of me—
murdered for refusing
to accept this slavery.

...Oh my daughter, Aïssatou,
when the rest of us
break free
I will have much to tell on your behalf.

There are hundreds
standing here upon the deck.
I cannot see the twelve
who were captured with me—
cannot find our warrior, Aly,
amid so many
forced into bondage
by mad men.

They bark all the time—
and the main man,
if he is to be considered a man at all,
growls like a jackal
and stalks like a demon.

He commands something
in his own language
and the others began to rush us
with buckets of water
the way you do common pigs—
the salt water scalding
the open wounds on our backs

where the toubob, just days ago,
burned with red hot irons
their accursed names
into our flesh.

As the crusted bile
and filth
fall from our nakedness
I see at the other end of my line
Aly, then one by one,
the other twelve—
All of them stone-faced and disbelieving.
Suddenly the whip snaps again
and we are forced to continue
to lockstep towards the death hole.

We move on
and there among the grief stricken
I see Fanta—medicine woman,
Healer of her village,
who during the recent plague
warded off diseases
with medicines and oblations
day and night,
never sleeping
except to dream the remedies.
Jackal-man has no idea—no idea.

He searches her frail body,
places his wretched hand upon her holy head
and pushes her at her mouth—no idea.

The man beside Fanta is Igbo.
He bears the scars of initiation on his cheek.
There is fire in his chest.
He is not from our village
but is no less defiant.
The whips crack again.
I turn to see fresh blood bursting
from the back of another man
who at this point only wants to live.
Jackal-man's helper, Dog Breath,
forces the poor man to fetch
more water to throw on us.

It is then that I hear HoHo, the village fool,
screaming at the top of his madness,
"Stop it, Toubob! Stop It!
Leave the dodo on my body!
You damn toubob want to take everything from me!"

Jackal-man unravels the leash
of the pale vicious dog
that is ever at his side
and HoHo scrambles back into place.

5

I move on,
feeling the unbearable pull at my ankles
and hearing the unforgettable cries
of those descending ahead of me.

Jackal-man
curses down at them
then shoves me
with the point of his gun
into the awesome hole.

The first day.

Illustration: Summoning Resolution

Igbo, Buman, Yoruba, Mandinka, Fulani.
There are at least these five.
They pray to the spirits, they curse the dogs.
There is no night, no day—
only timeless heaving here.

The boat bounces up and down up and down
leaving some sea-sick,
others sick with the flux,
still others planning death.
The ocean roars,
magnifying our fate
and I must force myself
to resist delirium.

...People! Bound but not broken!
We must not despair
but find a way to resist even now!
Where the toubob is taking us
there is no return—
we will never be among
our loved ones if we do not resist now!
We will be forever dismembered.
We must act deliberately, decisively
for already it has been one whole day
and the water leaves no path.
For the sake of ourselves,

for the sake of our children still at home,
we must find a way to take on the toubob.
If we die in the process, we die honorably
and shall return either way to our people.
If we overtake the toubob
we will have saved many nations.
Let our blood be spilled as sacrifice!
But let us seize hold of our destiny!

"Ashe!" Aly shouts
"Eyo! Ashe!" Fanta cries out from the end of the row.
And the many voices from other nations
rise up as well—
"Ashe! Queen Ramatoulaye! Ashe!"

Then Aly says,
"They will bring us back on deck
this night or the next so we should wait
for the opening and then come upon them
seven to one.
We should wait
until the one whom we call the Jackal
is present in order to destroy the head of the beast.
Use the irons to our benefit,
the stones, the teeth!
Set your freedom seeking eyes
upon whatever can be used as weapon.
As soon as you rise from the hole

check the landscape then wait
for the signal from our queen.
Wait for the 'now!' then take them!"

The second day
    or perhaps the third.

They do not open the hatch—
do not open the hatch.
We are as good as dead people
save for the betrayal of our senses.
We still taste the disgust
on our swollen tongues,
still feel the fecal slim
beneath our bodies
choking what little air remains.
We still feel the lice
biting, biting,
and the rats,
the awful rats.
The darkness thickens about us.
We wait, hearing heartbeat
and ocean, and the cries of our children
and the insanity of some who are already
raging against those chained beside them.
We wait
with little room to do more
than hope and wait.

They snatch the hatch open
and the first shaft of light
darts into the hole.
The Jackal and Dog Breath
yank at the chains.
We scoot out in broken rhythms

dragging and pushing out
the lifeless bodies
along with our own.

We emerge
into the jaundiced dusk
and find that four of us have died.
The mother of the wailing child.
A man who had refused to eat since leaving Goree Island.
A woman perhaps of heart failure.
And another man who simply willed himself dead.
Snake and another toubob
loosen the dead from among us
and without so much as a prayer,
without so much as a bowing of a wicked head,
or a fleeting thought of life, or of The Creator,
throw the bodies overboard to the trailing sharks
in four great splashes before us—
leaving the little girl's eyes stretched
in horror at the Snake.

"Momma!" she shrieks in a shock
almost drained of sound.
And that is all she speaks.
Her desperate eyes stuck staring at the spot
where they dumped her momma's body.

The toubob stroll the lines
making notes in their money books.
After they throw the water upon us
they throw food in tubs at our feet.

"Eat or you will not come up tomorrow!" Snake hisses.
Nobody knows what he is saying, of course.
He speaks in his own language.
But then the African one who is against us
and who acts at times as translator,
comes to back him up—

""Eat or you will not come up tomorrow!" he repeats
while gesturing to toss the gruel
into his most foul mouth.

HoHo leans in towards the food and smells it.
He jerks his face back and yells,
"Now I know what the toubob does with dodo.
He eats it!"

The African one slaps him.
"I told you to Shut Up!" he says
then turns to me,
"Eat!" he yells. "Eat!"

Eat what?!
Toubob beans?
Bad mush tainted with grease from forbidden pork?
Rotten stew smelling like everything else does of human waste—
The water, the wind! Everything tainted!
Eat what, toubob?
This fate you have designed for our African lives?
I will not!

I lift my head
in open defiance
and see, oh goodness, for the first time
that the land has disappeared.

There is no trace of my village
or the neighboring villages.
No dark earth, no giant baobab tree.
There is no trace of anything. Only water.
Water and sky, and the thin line that divides them.
The thin line between ancestors
and the unborn where we now stand.
It is so thin, so narrow
that it is almost non-existent.
But I make myself see it!
I will see you again, Aissatou!
I will not give up, my daughter!
I only wait for the appropriate time.

It is not now.

Jackal-man is here with us
but he is too expectant
and Dog-Breath is holding
too fast to his weapon.
It is not now.
I signal so with my head
and feel my flesh bleed
beneath the iron collar.

As I turn away from the waters
to look for what can be used as my weapon
I see two large speckled sea-birds
that have landed on the ship.
I look into the great dark eyes of one
and feel the spirit of great grandfather.
I look into the knowing gaze of the other
and recognize Nana through the pupils.

Oh Great Ones, help me!
Suddenly something charges through me
and I cannot move.
There are voices of my people
calling out from before
in this space.
Souls, wild and wandering,
wanting what?

Aly's gaze
draws me strongly.
His eyes say
"Now! Queen Ramatoulaye, Now!
The toubob are close enough to seize.
They will never, Oh Queen, be closer.
The time will never be more right!
Let us do it now!"

Not now, I say,
the words pulsing though my blood
before I even speak them.
Not yet.

The fourth day.

We are in the hovel
all day, all night.
And perhaps all day again.
Aly is consumed with rage.
Respect for me
is his only restraint.

"I am a warrior," he says,
"One who is willing to obey
even unto death
the authority of my leader.
One who wages war against opponents
of my people…"

Of course, his pledge has a dual purpose.
It assures me of his allegiance
and it strengthens his resolve
to carry out his oath.
The other twelve from various points
join in the pronouncement.

"I am a warrior—
One who is ready
to force into submission
whatever threatens the life of my people.
One who is willing to obey
even unto death
the authority of my leader."

When the trap door opens, we make our way out.
The one who is not with us loosens one of the crying children
and demands that he dance us.
We move with him, stiffly, watching
as one of the girls, not more than twelve years of age,
is loosened and dragged by the hair away from us.
She is badly frightened.
Snake's friends laugh and mimic her.
They stupidly buck their disgusting bodies as if in copulation.
They take her to the Jackal.
He opens the door,
the barking pale dog at his side,
and takes her in.

The women moan.
The men brace their backs.

"Dance!" Snake insists
while his beastly friends grab
their private parts and holler savagely.
They stalk the line
looking at each of the women,
the young and the old as well.
With one hand they hold guns
with the other
they fondle the women's breasts.

Is it not enough
that they have already humiliated us!
that they have stretched our mouths
and plunged their pig fingers
into our throats to examine out teeth!
that they have poked at our private parts
with pointed sticks
and forced some of the men and the women
to bend over and spread their cheeks
before their hateful gaze!
Is it not enough that the toubob Jackal
has taken into his cabin,
at this very moment,
a child of no more
than twelve rains,
with whom he intends to do his will!

Obviously not,
for now Dog Breath,
holding on to another one of our daughters,
forces his hand
between her trembling thighs
then jabs into her softness.
She cries out frantically
but to no avail.
He wraps his gunned hand around her waist
then forces his terrible toubob nakedness even harder into her.
He continues his dog-like movements

19

Illustration: Rape

while the rest of us ache in anger.
The one with crocodile skin
continues stalking us
to the rhythm of
Dog Breath's mounting grunts.
From one women to the next to the next,
the one with crocodile skin crawls
until he stops right before me.
The chains from my men rise instinctively.
I stand silent, without turning, without blinking—
then there, in the briefest instant,
behind his arrogant threat,
I see his cowardly retreat!
his inferior soul squirming there
behind dead gray eyes.

"Bitch!" he says defensively,
mad from the exposure.
Bitch!" he says again
lowering his gun to the stoop
and boldly cocking himself as the weapon.

"N-O-W!" Aly shouts in fury
and seven of the closest men charge upon the beast.
Seven others dart as quickly upon the snake.
The women from everywhere as far as their chains will allow

come vastly upon Dog-Breath with teeth, leg irons,
swollen fists, and ropes—
anything they can jab with!
I cannot reach the gun!
cannot reach the gun—
Bodies everywhere are fighting furiously
defying the chains, drawing blood.

Abruptly, fire explodes from the Jackal's gun.
"Get the hell up!" he shouts
"Damn Savage Heathens!"

Aly clutches the Snake more firmly
and the jackal points his gun straighter.

The African one who is not with us repeats,
"Get the hell up!"

But Aly is undaunted.
He stares right into the mouth of the gun
and with a warrior's mastery,
yanks Snake's twisted arms straight up from behind—
the bones cracking like dried limbs
from a draughted tree.
Now Snake really is a snake.
His arms are useless.

Using Snake as a human shield,

Aly moves towards the Jackal.

"Black bastard!"
the Jackal shouts.

"Go to hell," Aly smarts.

"Get him, you ignoramuses!" the Jackal yells
and at that, Dog-Breath and the Crocodile
and the one who is not with us
and another young one I had never even seen
before that moment,
all come upon Aly to kill him.

Another shot rings out—
this time for the others.
I imagine the Jackal says,
"Don't kill him, you idiots!
This one is my gold."
They look outdone by the notion.
Shaking his head in disgust
the Jackal signals for them
to put us back down below
and walks away.

Once his door is closed
the others come upon Aly

knocking him to the ground—
kicking their thick boots hard into his back,
his stomach, his groin, his helpless face,
leaving his eyes like entrails
from a slaughtered calf—
then turning to the other men,
they crack, oh they crack
their merciless whips
until blood
blood
blood.

Then they drag Aly's mangled body
away from most of his warriors
to a position in the middle
right next to me.

The fifth day.

The darkness throbs.
The young woman who was violated
bangs her head unceasingly
against the floor
Uh
The child who lost her mother
cries even louder now
Uh
And the men
who were beaten
uh uh
groan beyond words

And Aly's breathing
is just unbearable
"Ah-h-h..."
The words I hear from him now
are the first in hours—

"My Creator,
strengthen my body! Ah-h-h
Make me whole ah-h-h
Once more! Ah-h-h.
Make my body...ah-h-h..."

The sixth day.
There is no seventh—

25
Only this long, long night.

They bring us on deck
and toss three more into the water.
Creator receive them.
I do not know their names.

Aly is straining to keep standing.
His eyes are still swollen shut.
And in the place of his branding
I can see maggots crawling through the pus.
As I reach up to wipe them away
I see that they are also
feeding on the blood from my own wrists.

The other warriors are starring
into the fading sun—
searching perhaps for some hint
of the sirius star
that could help guide us home.

Nobody looks into the eyes
of the toubob—
It is too soon to face again such evil.

The twelve year old, Amina,
who has been with the Jackal
comes limping from his quarters—

her weak, buckling legs
streaked with blood and semen.
Without even once looking our way
the poor child breaks for the edge of the boat,
climbs upon the nets,
then whirls her violated body
into the blue.

"No-o-o!" Dog Breath and the Jackal
yell bitterly into the foaming waters.

And the idiot one who is not with says,
"A thousand slave dollars
gone to the damn sharks."

The eighth day.

The one who is not with us
is a coward.
I cannot tell what nation he is from,
he is so much one of them.
He walks like they do.
He talks like they do.
His body bears the same toubob arrogance
but defers in their presence.
He smells of rum and his eyes are devilish.
He has shamed his father and mother.
His name is best unknown.
His family would be dishonored—is dishonored.
He watches me watch him.
I see him reiterate their words.
I see him interpret our looks
and our expressions to them.
I even see him translate our silences, varied and vast.
I see him tell our hiding places.
See him turn us over to them
again and again
for private gain and pitiful swig of rum.
I will remember this one who is not with us.
His presence like the toubob's must be remembered.

The ninth day.

Great Grandfather!
Nana!
You have come to help us?
...What is this you are saying?

"You are destined to come
into the land of the toubob," they say.
"You are being sent
to perform the truth of freedom.
Go bravely."

What!?
What!?
Such a burden is impossible!
There is no way to perform freedom
among these beasts!
This is impossible!

"What is the Queen saying?"
I hear in the darkness from Aly.
"The Queen must be dreaming?"

I surely must be.
I cannot bear this.

The tenth day.

29

...Being sent?

No
No No No No.

The eleventh day.

There is a singer on board the ship.
Not in this row but adjacent us
about five people down.
She is gifted with songs in the old way.
They are not the traditional songs
but rise up out of groaning
and transform magically into comfort.
It is a groaning a mother makes
at the beginning of labor perhaps
or one that a night wind makes when it is full
of ancestral voices.

The singer calls herself Bamidele,
Come-Home-With-Me, Bamidele.
Bamidele only speaks in song
and only after the day is spent
and the hours have passed
and the water has been thrown
and the weeping for home begins again.

First she sings of water, then of sun, then of seeds.
It is not so much the words but the sound resisting despair.
She sings of baby crying from a basket, of food
left burning on the fire. She sings of cowry shells
tossed upon a mat, of dark fingers dipping into fufu, of
ringdoves in the distant night. She sings of red birds swarming
around a compound, of mothers wailing onto the ground,
of fathers looking through telling waters at a ship sailing

silently away. She sings of aunties
making groundnut stew, of uncles planting yams.
Bamidele sings of tall swaying palm trees
and the smell of the rich dark earth.

And I think of you, Aissatou,
in the bright morning sun
when last I braided your beautiful hair
and felt your breath upon my knee.

The twelfth day.

Another child has gone
to be among the ancestors.
Our Creator rest his soul.
He was about seven years of age.
He had begun to take to the one who is not with us,
to respond to his slight attentions---
desperate as he was for comfort.
This child was the one whom they used to dance us.
His young lungs began to fill with phlegm
and over the harshest days,
his wheezing got worse and worse.
He could not discern
that this African one who is not with us
was against his life.

This traitor had cupped the boy's head at times,
rubbing it the way he had seen the toubob do for luck.
Who knows—perhaps even grooming the boy
for a position not unlike his own.

This boy who has gone on
was not like the one called Dash
who is also about his age.

Dash looks up to Aly, emulates his every move,
squats like he does before his food,
fixes his face like he does before the sun
when first coming out of the hole.

And he looks at the toubob with the same disgust.
Completely different than the one
who has now gone on.

Perhaps the one who has gone on
has been spared a fate
worse than death.

The thirteenth day.

The singer is singing tonight.
Suni is adding the drum of his voice.
Bump Bump—Bump Bump—Bump Bump
inspiring Bamidele to get bolder
Another warrior joins in with the chop of his chains,
then the pound of the feet
Yeah from the other side another beat
Fists banging, banging
Sound coming strong
Voices mounting, mounting
Uh-huh mounting on
Like a body
Come to life
this sudden song
From the depths of the death pit
the spirit striving on
Then
"Stop that noise! You Black bastards!"
the Jackal yells down into the darkness..
"Stop that noise. You pile of shit!"

Fourteenth day.

Aly turns towards me.
"Queen Ramatoulaye,
Our Creator is restoring my strength.
Already the soreness
is leaving my body.
In another day or two
we will succeed."

"We will succeed!" comes a young voice
through the darkness
It is the child, Dash,
whose spirit
is wounded with Aly's own.

The fifteenth day.

We come above board.
The African one who is not with us
comes upon Dash,
loosens him from the chains
and signals for him to dance us.
He wants us to stretch our limbs
and make our blood move
but the boy refuses.

"Traitor!" Dash shouts defiantly
"Big Tooth, dodo-head traitor!"

HoHo is already renewed by this
but Aly intervenes—
"Do as he says, Dash!
Dance us. Lift your arms.
Raise your legs.
Dance us.
Do not provoke him young warrior.
Dance us. I command you!"

Dash obediently lifts his legs
never taking his tear filled eyes from Aly.
He slowly takes the position of the cobra,
then the tiger,
then the lion.
We follow, untangling our poor bodies
from the painful stiffness.

Dog Breath is not satisfied.
He cracks the whip at the boy's head.
But Dash, determined not to act threatened,
begins to lift his slight arms before us
into a full eagle's spread
and he stays there until the aching arms of Aly
are at last parallel to his own.

The sixteenth day.

We will succeed!
We will seize their weapons.
Do not hesitate to take them.
Let this be the day
for our enemies to meet their maker!

The seventeenth day.

We come on deck ready.
It has been ten or more days since the attack
and we are ready.
They are cautious of us.
They know that we have not been broken.
Dog Breath and the African one who is not with us
and the young one whom we had never seen before the fight
all stand glaring with their guns.

Four of them descend into the hole
to scrub the quarters with vinegar and tar.
Their faces are covered with cloth masks
but we can still hear them gagging from the stench.

But it is our turn to breathe now
and to watch for an opening
in the toubob's defense.

One of them approaches one of our men
and with a sharp iron tool,
begins to scrap the bile and scales
from his weakened body.

The man draws fiercely away
but Dog Breath forces him
to endure the tortuous scraping.

As we continue to watch
every corner of the boat
who would suddenly appear
for the first time since the fight
but the mummified reptile
all wrapped in slings of bed sheets!

"A dead man!" HoHo yells
pointing to the Snake.
"A Dead man! Ha!
He is entombed!
He awaits a soul!
Zombie!
Za-Za-Zombie!"

The indignant Snake ignores HoHo
and marches directly towards Aly
intending to retaliate I am sure.

But Dash, who has been loosened to dance us,
flings his ready-aimed body
into the back of Snake's legs
making him land on his broken arms,
and scream out like a wounded hyena!

And then little Bamidele, oh dear,
drags Snake into our reach, yes!
and one of Aly's army,

triumphantly gives us once again
the sound
of the breaking twig.
Crack!
And for the first time
in I don't know how long
all of us just break down and laugh and laugh and laugh.

The Jackal rushes in
upon the unexpected scene, saying,
"What did I tell you men about your foolishness?...
And what in the hell happened
to your legs?"

The nineteenth day.

"We must succeed another way,
Queen Ramatoulaye.
We must find another way
to free ourselves."

Suppose, Aly, that we are destined
to complete this journey?

"What?"

That we are destined to stand
upon the ground of the toubob."

"Our Creator forbid this."

But what if Our Creator would allow such a thing
and still call us to perform the truth of freedom?

"What are you saying. Queen Ramatoulaye?
that we are to subject ourselves to this degradation?"

No, Aly—
I'm not suggesting submission
but a demonstration of freedom's worth.
If we are destined to stand upon the tubob grounds
let us leave there for all to witness
an everlasting remembrance
of our resistance.

You mean an embrace of death
as resistance to enslavement?
Eyo! Queen Ramatoulaye, Ashe!"

Let us all go back through the water
each and every one
chanting "you can't chain the spirit!
You can't chain the sun"

"You can't chain the spirit!" they echo
"You can't chain the sun!"

"You can't chain the spirit!
You can't chain the sun!"

"You can't chain the spirit!"—

"But!"
comes a voice
familiar and challenging
"Is there no other way
to win this battle than by beating them
to the death act?"

It is Suma, one of Aly's army.

"Yes!" comes another voice from the darkness.

"Perhaps once on the toubob's soil
we can overtake them!"

"True," cries another one,
"We can resist them, or prove our worth to them."

What?!

"Yes, then they will grant us freedom
just like we do those who have been in our service!"

Nonsense! Absolute Nonsense!
Have you not looked into the eyes of the Snake?
Have you not seen the greed and treachery
in the eyes of the jackal!
Or witnessed the hatred and lust rise from Dog Breath!?
No, my fine warrior,
these are not men given to human compassion.
Their hearts are hardened.
Our sister tells us that the Jackal,
after he takes her,
prays to his god for forgiveness
and then weeps when he is not heard.
And she says that the African one who is not with us
laughs at her fate.
He says that our God
and the toubob's God
have abandoned the boat!

that they are the gods now
and that we are at their mercy!
But we are not.

Look at the one with crocodile skin!
Surely you know where those scars came from.
They are brandings from hot irons
intended for the flesh of some African
who managed to sear
upon the toubob's own face
an indelible sign of African resistance—
a sign of encouragement, my dear warriors,
to be witnessed by whom ever
would have to confront
this so-called enslaver in the future.
We, my people,
must accomplish at least as much.
We must leave our mark
on the toubob's land!
We will walk the water!
That is the best way for us to fight.

"Queen Ramatoulaye,
this is not like you
nor is it like King Mawdo—
     The Creator rest his soul.
Although we are slaves, we can still resist—

We can still hope!"

"Suma!" Aly shouts
"You will not address us as slaves!"

"Slaves?!" HoHo repeats. "Slaves!?"

"What else are we?
Our legs are chained, our hands are bound.
We live in darkness, we eat waste,
we move to their every command,
they beat us with whips, rape our women,
knee us, Aly, in our groans
and desecrate our dead.
We, Aly, are slaves!"

"Slaves?" HoHo says again.

"Not so, Suma, and
you will not address us as such
in my presence or in the presence of our queen.
We are Africans who have been captured--
Africans with a way of life
that has sustained generations.
You, Suma, are not only disrespectful to our traditions.
You are insubordinate!"

"Said the slave
who would-be master!"

"Your challenge must be accepted, Suma.
We cannot afford this break among us
or the possibility
of you drawing the weak to your way of thinking.
We, all of us, will take to the water
as soon as we touch ground.
I obviously am not in a position—"

"Truly—"

"to take you on myself
but there are warriors
within an arm's reach of your windpipe
whose strong swift hands can extinguish your treason
and leave you dead!
Stay awake as a lion, my brother.
Do not blink."

"Slaves..." HoHo whispers. "Slaves..."
The twenty-first day.

We come out of the hole
and stand on deck.
The clouds are so very low
that we are able to touch them.
The bodies of those in the distance
fuse with the mist.
We are already it seems
becoming spirit.
The toubob are uneasy
with our presence.
They probe their guns
into the crowd.
The one who is not with us dares to come closer.
Even his dark eyes cannot read our faces, our masks.

The twenty-second day
    or perhaps the twenty-eighth day.

The Jackal wants another woman.
He nods towards us.
The one with Crocodile skin grabs Aisha
and pushes her to him.

The zombie is nowhere to be found.
The young toubob who appeared during the fight
keeps his distance with his gun.
He is the Jackal's son, I hear.
The one who is not with us is here as well.
He waits until the Jackal closes the door
then starts to strut about.

At first No-with-us seems
to be taunting Suma
but then it is easy to see
that he is mimicking the Jackal
to the amusement of Crocodile.
He toots out his fat belly
just like the Jackal does,
puckers his mouth into a point and gr-o-w-ls
just like the Jackal does.
Crocodile falls over laughing at the Jackal's likeness
and the one who is not with us
feeds on the foolishness.

He continues prancing and prancing
until he stops dead in front of Fanta, the healer.
First, he sniffs at the air over her head
and then into her sweating armpits.
He pretends initially to be knocked over by the odor
then pretends to crawl spellbound back up into it.
He comes dreadfully closer, his throbbing nostrils
almost touching her blackness
then suddenly, powerfully,
Fanta fixes her small veined hand
before his startled eyes and declares,
"he who dishonors his ancestors
curses himself!"

Stung for a moment
he tries to shake it off
but it is too heavy upon him.

"Come on," Crocodile laughs wickedly,
wanting the mimicry to continue.
He even grabs one of our youngest sons
and pretends to copulate with him.
"Come on," he laughs to keep the foolishness going.

But the one who is not with us
can no longer laugh.

The thirty-second day.

What was Fanta doing when they came upon her?

Going to another's home
to deliver another child?
Tending a dying elder?
Gathering leaves in the bush?
Washing clothes?
Lying with her husband?

...Mawdo...

The thirty-third day.

There is fierceness
in the distance.
A struggle for sure.

Men are scrounging and fighting in the dark.
Voices from either side
spontaneously begin to pronounce
the warrior pledge
drowning out the cries of the children.

"I am a warrior!" they chant.
"One who is willing to obey
even unto death
the authority of my leader!
One who wages war
against the opponents of my people."

In the breaks of the chant I can hear
poor Suma struggling for his life.

"One who is trained to kill with weapons
or bare hands."

He is gasping for breath.
The men go on.

"One who is ready to force into submission

whatever threatens the life of my people."

It is done.
Over.
Oh Creator receive his soul.

The thirty-fourth day.

Illustration: Extinguishing Treason

We scoot from the darkness
and Aly watches for the dead body of Suma
to be dragged from the pit.

But this surely is a reversal of fate
for Suma himself rises triumphant from the hole
and throws the dead body of Aly's best warrior
onto the waiting floor.

"There!" he roars
over his defeated foe.
"There!"

The thirty-fifth day.

"All of us
will not walk the water
when we touch the ground!"
Suma shouts
once we are back in the darkness.
"I will not submit to death!
It does no good for me.
This is not the way of my people.
You are not my enemy, Aly..."

"Says who?" HoHo interjects.

"It is not you whom I have vowed to fight..."

"Ha! He did not blink!"

"I am not in disobedience to the queen.
I am in obedience to a higher law...."

"Stay awake as a lion!"

"that demands her protection.
It is the healer's hand that fixes
and the warrior's hand that strikes!"

"And," Aly finally speaks up,
"It is the queen's hand that rules."
"No my fine warrior

No my fine warrior
No my fine warrior," HoHo chants.

"Let me put it like this,"
Suma insists,
"Most of those who are going along
with your backward way of thinking
are chained here with you
in this short line.
And as long as I am here
on this short line with you
there will be
No walking the water.
I will resist you,
your warriors,
Queen Ramatoulaye
and who ever else
with all my God-given strength!"

Aly is incensed
and says
"Call it what you will,
you donkey's asshole!
We will leave though the water!"

Thirty-sixth day.

Fanta is speaking to Dash
and he keeps asking why? why?

I strain to hear what she is saying.
I think we all do
and find that she has transformed herself
into Anansi the spider.

"In the time of the famine
The king called on Jalee Mamadou
to help lift the spirits of the people," Fanta says wearily.
"Jalee Mamadou had spoken on many occasions
and it is from his mouth that I learned this traditional tale."

"Ashe!" HoHo says wanting her to go on.

"There were seven children
that Anansi had," Fanta continues.
"Some say they were all seven of them sons
but I know that there must have been four sons
and three daughters."

"But Momma Fanta," Dash says,
"What difference does that make?
And why are you changing the tale?"

"Hush Child," Fanta chides moving to the next words,
"The first child's name was See Far

because she could—"

"See far," Dash says
trying to bear with the tale.

"And the second child's name
was Road Builder
because?"

"...Because he could build roads," Dash says.

"And the third child's name was Drink Water—"

"because he could swallow the entire ocean
and hold it in his mouth
for a long long time."

"Right, Dash, you are.
And the fourth child was Fish Carver
because he could carve well into the flesh of the fish,
and the Fifth child, Stone Thrower
could throw all the way up to the sky.
And the sixth child whose name was Cushion
could turn himself into a cushion all soft and tender."

"You, Brother Aly, would do well
to listen again to this soft and tender tale."

"Go to hell, Suma!"

"Now one day," Fanta continued,
"See Far said, 'Oh, I see the Father is in trouble!'
but he was far far away.
At once Road-Builder began building a road
that would lead to him.
And just as they had traveled the road they ran into a river.
Drink Water, of course, drank it all up
and there in the bed of the river
they saw Anansi
struggling inside the stomach
of the great great fish.
The fish indeed had swallowed him—
had swallowed him whole!"

"Well, Fish Carver immediately pulled out his enormous knife
and began carving the flesh of the fish
to get Anansi out.
He carved and he carved and he carved
until Anansi was finally free."

"But as soon as Anansi was free,
down swooped this huge, incredible bird
and lifted him up in the cup of his beak
and flew with him off into the sky."

"And 'Oh no you don't!' cried Stone Thrower.

And he picked out a stone and with all of his might
threw it at the incredible bird
whose mouth flung open letting Anansi fall
and Cushion, he spread himself out as far as he could and
dear Anansi landed right on top of him."

"DID Not," Suma interjected,
"crawl back into the river and die!"

And another voice rang out in support of Suma,
"Did not curse the stone thrower for throwing the stone!"

And that's when I spoke up—
And did not cut off the head of See Far
for seeing that Anansi was in deep trouble!

"Queen Ramatoulaye
you do not have to dignify his comments
with your response!
And as for the traitor who joins him—

"What?" Suma replies
"He should guard his windpipe, right?
He should not blink, let me guess."

"Anyway," Fanta continues,
when Anansi brushed himself off

and stood up before his children who had saved his life,
he realized that he wanted

to do something special for them."
"So he decided to give them in appreciation
this beautiful ball of shimmering gold.
But suddenly, Dash, they all began to bicker
over who deserved it most.
'I was the one who saw you in trouble,' said one,
"so I should get the reward!'
'Well I was the one who built the road
that led us to you, Father—'
'Well me, I drank up the whole ocean
and held it in my mouth!'
'I took my knife and carved the fish,
which nobody else could do.'
'It was my stone, dear Papa,
that knocked that huge, bird in the mouth!'
and Cushion just sat there smiling saying over and over again
'hey, you know what I did for you.'"

"With all due respect, Fanta. That boy, Cushion, is me!"

"Ha!"

"Anyway," Fanta continues,

"Poor Anansi didn't know what to do.
How to reward the gifted, yet very selfish children,
so he went to inquire of Our Creator.
And do you know what Our Creator told Anansi?"

"What?" Bambidele whispers.

"Our Creator told him not to break the ball into seven pieces—
not to break the ball at all
but to take the shimmering ball high up in the sky,
set it there for all to see."

"but what is the ball?" Dash asks. "Is it the sun?"

"It is truth.
And you can't chain it, Dash," Aly says,
"you can't chain the sun."

"Somebody's going to have to set it through," Fanta insists
"Somebody's going to have to make it a shinning example
for all the others to see."

"Not so," Suma disagrees.
"The ball is indeed the sun, Dash,
but it's already set.
All we have to do
is lift our dull African faces and see it."

"Dash," Bamidele says softly,
"We really have not gotten to that part of the tale.
We have only seen trouble
and drank a river full of tears.."

"This one calling herself Bamidele is mad!"
somebody says from the other end.

"Leave Bamidele alone," HoHo rebuts.

Thirty-fifth day
...if I haven't said that already.

Who did you leave behind?
I ask Aly.

"My wife, I left behind
and my son,
first born.
My father, still strong.
My Mother, my mother.
I left behind an older brother,
whom, as you know, works in your service also
and three sisters,
younger sisters,
of marrying age—
two who were killed in the march
to the castle,
and cousins,
almost two dozen cousins.
A whole village,
Queen Ramatoulaye,
A whole village."

Thirty- sixth or thirty-seventh day.

We limp from the hole
and after they have given us food
Crocodile makes Dash dance us.
He stands first as a crane,
and we all follow,
then as a tiger
and we all follow.
Then as an eagle.
Straining against the power of the pain
we spread our wings high over our heads
and lift until we are beyond—
beyond the water and the white bones below
beyond the toubob's boat and all the stench—
beyond the toubob, beyond beyond

"Wow..." the young toubob says
and we land again on the boat—
the flying Dash, transforming back
into a dusty boy
in chains.

The young toubob,
without thinking, leads Dash to be chained
to a spot other than his own
but immediately
the crocodile objects.

Not-with-us backs him up,
"Do not ever
move from your position!" he says
mouthing the words
as if we ourselves can not understand
our own African tongue.

Then he checks his book again
to confirm our designated positions,
as if his very world would fall
if ever this order was disturbed.

Huh—
We have already flown free
of this toubob order of yours, Not-with-us!
Write that in your little money book!

Another day.

They bring us on deck.
The young toubob is stretching into each face
looking for Dash.
He unfastens Dash even while he is eating
and waits eagerly for him to dance us.

Dash turns only to Aly.

When it is time to dance
the young toubob poises himself
to imitate our movements.

Dash sees this and so we dance
but we do not fly this day.

And while we dance,
we suffer Suma's taunting.
"I am sharpening myself for survival!
I am sharpening myself for life!
A mean, fish-carving, wicked blade--
I am the knife!

Dreamer to his soul.

Thirty-eighth day.

"I hear that rats rush themselves off cliffs
in droves
to taper off their numbers,"
Suma says slowly.
"Is that the idea, Aly?"

The thirty-eighth or thirty-ninth day.

"We do not need more water drinkers!
We do not need to drown ourselves for freedom!
Look at all those who have gone that way before us—
There was the young sister who threw herself overboard—
and this young one's mother
who was tossed before her very eyes—
and the dozens whom the toubob
dumped when their beaten bodies
could no longer bear it!" Suma shouts into the darkness.

At this the children start weeping again
but Suma is relentless.
"The floor of this ocean is filled with bones
of the ancestors who had to go this way.
We do not need any more water drinkers!
We need somebody to carve Father from the fish!"

"Yeah, Yeah, Yeah! Great Alpha YaYa!" Aly says beside me.
"Great Ancestral Voice of Stupidity!" he mocks.

I say nothing.
I know that Suma is as powerless as the rest of us are
to make even the first necessary scratch
upon this giant fish that has swallowed
our hope for deliverance.
The fortieth day.

Eight weeks,
he says
eight weeks.
Not six but eight weeks
we have been on the water.
That's what Not-with-us says,
though he will not answer Suma's question
of how long the journey actually is.
Eight times seven.

The fifty-sixth day.

The woman/child—
the one who was taken by Dog Breath
that first week while we stood and witnessed—
the one who banged her head incessantly
for almost three days afterwards
is vomiting over her food.
Vomiting uncontrollably—
heaving now, now settling
and wiping her tears away.
The women quiet themselves
to an awesome silence.
The men look away.
We descend into the hole
without a word.

The fifty-eighth day.

Illustration: Heaving Flesh

We ascend and the smell is enough!
It stretches its ghost hands
down into her throat and into her belly
and wraps its fingers
around her guts.
The women closest to her
reach out to comfort.

"All of you spread out!"
Not–with–us yells,
"And I mean, do it now!" he adds.

Our poor daughter is left there on the floor,
a bundle of heaving flesh.

Fifty-ninth day.

"What is wrong with me?"
our daughter screams in the middle of the night.
"What is wrong, Oh Creator, with me?
Somebody talk to me please.
Nana Fanta, healer, please!
What is wrong?"

"Child, It is I, Fanta.
What is your name?"

"Fatou, Nana, Fatou."

"And rightly so, my child.
Rightly so."

"What do you mean, Nana?"

The women moan in unison.

"What is wrong with me, Nana?"

"Child of Africa,
you are bearing
the toubob's seed—
the first child of this passage."

"No...."

"Yes," Fanta says
and we can hear Fatou weeping.

"What can I do, Nana?"

And before she answers
Suma and Aly raise their voices.

"This is an abomination," Aly shouts.
"A violation
not only of the girl
but upon all our people as well.
They will not desecrate our bodies,
rape our women,
and force their seed to feed on our blood!
Fatou, even though you are not in this line,
you must, young daughter,
not allow this wretchedness to continue.
You must find a way once upon the toubob shores
to free yourself and come before The Almighty."

"Just fine," Suma interjects.
"Like the girl has not been wounded enough
without pressure now to walk, plump bellied and all,
headlong into the ocean to plead her case
before Almighty God, who is, all along, seeing exactly
what has befallen her.
Fatou does not have to walk on water."

"She is bearing water, even as we speak.
The child inside her is as much hers
as it is the wretched toubob's.
She does not have to kill herself
to find release."

"You're a fool, Suma."

"You've forgotten that you are a slave!" someone shouts.

"Africans who are captured," Aly yells.

"Idiots All," Fanta shouts.

"Toubob's seed in the belly of the babe?"
Hoho says as if trying to grasp the notion.
He says it again, this time beginning to cry.
"...belly of the babe?.."

"My daughter, how are you?" Fanta asks.

"I don't know.
I never had a baby before.
I-I might have even felt it move
last night.
My Momma was,
is having

A baby at home—
Queen Ramatoulaye?"

"Yes child?"

"What would you do?"

"Fatou,
Innocent Fatou.
I would pray
and cry some more.
And when the time was ripe
I would gladly endure
whatever in order to love her
in the way that's best."

"But what is that way, Queen Ramatoulaye?'

I do not answer right away.

"Queen Ramatoulaye?"

For me
it is to go back through the water.
For you it may be a different story.

The sixtieth day and the sixty-second.

"I, too, am carrying a child,"
comes a voice out of the darkness.
"Although I conceived before being captured
and I bear the seed of my husband
I understand, Fatou, why you might
not want to kill your child."

"And I understand
why you might feel that you must!" says another.

The sixty-fourth day.

I am ill.
It could be an illness of sympathy
but I feel it none the less.
And it is not only me.
The other women and some of the men
are ill as well.
It could be bad food.
It could be just bad.

The fifty-fifth day and the fifty-sixth.

This is the third day
that I am vomiting.
I taste bile
and blood.
The sixty-seventh day.

We come from the hole
and the Jackal peers hard into our eyes
and lifts a stick to check our mouths.
He makes the others rush our fever with water.
Our poor bodies shiver helplessly.

The sixty-eighth day.

"I am dying,"
a voice cries out.
"My soul will meet you at home."

It is one of the men
from Fanta's village.
Tutu.
Our Creator rest his soul.

The sixty-ninth day.

The fever
has intensified.
Our people are convulsing—
 another three have gone on—
Creator...

The seventieth day.

We struggle up
out of the hole--
wet our mouths with water.
Our poor bodies languishing.
Aisha is blind....

The seventy-first day.

The Jackal is anxious.

His eyes are wide and uncertain.

His mouth is covered with a mask.

He brings a bowl

of some potion.

Not-with-Us makes us drink it.

One after the other.

It is bitter like wormwood

or goldenseal.

Oh Creator,

Wave over this potion.

Ashe.

The seventy-second day.

Twelve more among us
have died,
I think.
the seven-third?

  no, seventy-seventh day

I think
rest their souls.

the seventy-something day.

Illustration : Unspeakable Misery

Mawdo?
Dear.
Your face is beautiful, Mawdo.
Allow me
to touch you
touch you.
Do not draw from me.
Mawdo...

You damn toubob want to take everything!..

Except to dream the remedies...

The unbearable pull at my ankles...

without so much as a bowing of a wicked head...

Rotten stew smelling
like everything else does of human waste...
Eat what, Toubob!?
Eat what?
This fate you have designed for our African lives, I will not!...

hunching
hideous hunching—body lice—
while the rest of us ache in anger—
Bitch!

Their toubob names burned on our African backs!

Make—me—whole!...
Oh Aissatou!...

You are destined to come
into the land of the toubob...
No-o-o!

Bitch!
Unbearable, wicked head, hunching...

Is there no other way to win this battle
than by beating them—you have come to help us? --
to the death act?

You are being sent... being sent..

I took my knife and carved the fish,
which nobody else could do—
carve the fish.
fecal slim
carve the fish
no baobab tree,
carve!
carve!

how?...

I awaken to the darkness
and the sound of the hatch being opened.
My fever has broken.
I am so dizzy
I can hardly stand.
The memories and voices
are still slouching in my head.

How would anyone in their right mind begin
to even want to carve father
from this wretchedness!

I look at Aly.
His body is skeletal.
Fanta is even more frail.
Dash is but a bone.
Suma and Fatou are pitiful.
Twelve more of us gone

Bamidele looks back at me
and whispers,
"Our Creator, Our Creator
has spared us."

I do not answer back
but slowly lift the mush to my mouth.

"How much longer is the journey?"

I hear Suma ask
in a voice that doesn't even sound like his own.
It is raspy and broken and he coughs so much
that it is hard to listen.
"How long?" he asks again.

Not-with-us says
"the journey is 105 days.
You have at least twenty-one days more to go.

Crocodile intervenes asking
what did Suma say?
But Not-with-us
walks away.

We drag ourselves back down into the hole.
The eighty-fourth day.

"Nana Fanta?"

"Yes Fatou?"

"In my fever I dreamed
I was on the land of the toubob.
Two big hands
snatched my baby from me.
It was so horrible a thing."

"Perhaps it was just a dream,"
moans the woman who is also carrying a child.

"I dreamed,"
Suma says,
"I had entered
the toubob's land.
I was digging...the earth.
along with other men.
Perhaps I was even beneath the earth
a dead man.
I distinctly remember the smell of earth."

He coughs
uncontrollably
then goes on.

"And you, Queen,
what did you dream?"

And what was I to say?
that I dreamed this incessant nightmare
that we live daily? —
that my people were set adrift
on this ocean of tears
without hope of ever being free? —
that my dead husband came to me
and would not allow me to even touch his freedom!? —
that the voices of the ancestors
in every little swish
call out to me, "carve father,
carve father from the fish!"

Suma, my brother,
if I thought there was the slightest hope,
the most meager sign
that we could begin to carve Father
from this wretched fish
I would abandon the walk,
but there is no sign Suma,
no hope that we will ever be able
to determine our destiny
or hold fast to our dignity as human

among these toubob.

"Let me give you a sign,
Queen Ramatoulaye.
Let me try.
Put me to the test—
nothing spectacular—
just something,
anything that can give us
a measure of hope.
You choose the challenge,
Queen Ramatoulaye.
You choose, and if I am unable
to meet your challenge
then by my soul's honor,
I will gladly walk the water
along with this entire line."

Suma, I will not make it easy for you.
I will not give our people
a false sense of possibility.

"I agree, Queen Ramatoulaye."

Very well, then Suma.
Given the toubob's determination to keep us
in our designated positions,

your challenge is to get the toubob
to move you from this short line

onto one of the long lines away from us.
Let us see you achieve
even that small measure of control
and we will take this as a sign of hope.

"Ashe." Suma says, coughing loudly again. "Ashe."

Aly is absolutely still.
And so is everyone else.
Eighty-fifth day.

Illustration: A Measure of Hope

We come from the hole.
The Jackal strolls the line
much more settled than before
but still poking his medicine stick
and looking at his money book.
He turns and without a word to anyone
goes back to his quarters.

Before we are sent back down below
Suma finds that
our calculations are way off.
We do not have twenty days
but only seven or eight at most.
The Liars!
According to their young one,
who Suma is too busy priming,
this journey is almost passed.

Seven days left or eight.

We come from the hole.
Suma lifts his head as if praying
then waits until both Not-with-us
and Crocodile are within hearing range.

He addresses Not-with-us.

"Sir," Suma says submissively
"If I could be allowed to say a word?"

Not-with-us simply looks at him.

"It is the storm, Sir," he says.

It is too much for me to witness Suma,
a warrior so full of manhood,
debase himself in this manner.

"Whenever the storm comes heavy
as these skies are promising now,
the tilting of the boat down below is so sever
that all we can do is keep from drowning, Sir.
If I could be moved
from the end here to perhaps the other side?"

Crocodile leans forward, as is his custom,
and waits for Not-with-us to translate

but Not- with-us, ignores Crocodile.

"What do you take me for, a fool!"
Not- with-us says to Suma.
"You think I don't know you
have some plan in your dumb mind?
Do I look stupid, you bastard?!"

"Oh no, Sir, Not you.
You are the one with authority
to determine our condition.
I am reduced to this condition.
You are not.
I simply request your indulgence."

Crocodile leans more anxiously between the two.
Not- with-us ignores him.

"I know you only want to stage some trick!" he says.

"No, I swear this is not so.
It is the water," Suma gasps.
"Sometimes the water
is at least up to the back of my ears!"

"What the hell is he saying?"
Crocodile shouts.

"I can handle this!" Not-with-us insists.
But Crocodile,

turns away from Not-with-us
to address Suma himself.
"What the hell did you say?!"

And Suma with the same humble tone as before
and in the same African tongue
which Crocodile still cannot comprehend, says—

"I am asking, Toubob,
to be moved from here to over there
to avoid being drowned in the night waters."
And he ends his request with his ironed wrists
extended well before him.

"Oh!" says Crocodile.
"You want to go there?"

"I told him No!"
Not-with-us insists.

But the crocodile
dismissively reaches for his keys
and mumbles to Not-with-us
something like

"You're as wretched as they are,
you black bastard!"

The crocodile has no idea
the extent of the insult.
Not-with-us, who up to this point,
has treasured the illusion
of being embraced as one of them,
suddenly pounces upon the crocodile
with a fierceness of a tiger.
The fighting becomes so violent
that Dog Breath abandons his post,
Snake drags in from where ever he was
and the Jackal flings wide open his door.

"What the fuck is going on here?" he yells
and, seeing that two of his own crew are at war,
he decides to let them continue.

"The winner will decide the move!"
Not-with-us growls.

This is too ironic, really!
If the toubob beats him,
we win.
If he beats the toubob,
we still have not lost.

Crocodile says something about
dumb-ass niggers
and Not-with-us goes wild.

He flips the crocodile
on his back and in a flurry of blows,
bloodies the crocodile's branded face
to an appearance of pounded liver.
The crocodile then somehow wrestles
into a position of dominance,
grabs Not-with-us around the neck
and begins choking the life-breath from his twisted body
but to no benefit.

Not-with-us flips him over again
and stands him blow for blow.

The young one, the son,
who is seldom on deck
is horrified.

"Stop them!" he shouts "Stop them!"
But the Jackal will not do it.

By now I am fully aware
that Suma had not expected Not-with-us
to grant his request at all.

In fact, his strategy
depended on the certainty
of that denial.
Suma was exposing, and undermining
the implicit chain of authority.

Our warrior had played
upon the toubob's need
to be informed and in control.
In making a request
which he knew Not-with-us would not grant,
he had triggered the toubob's fears
about being excluded from our African talk.
And now the two so-called masters
were in a most fierce entanglement
which could go either way.

"Sniff now, Not-with-us!"
one of our warriors shouts
leaning closer upon the two.

"Yeah, you hyena's ass!" another woman joins in.

"Good for nothing, white-on-the-inside yam-man!"
another yells.

"Baboon's dung!"

"No, Snake shit!" Fatou screams
holding her swollen womb.

Then from out of nowhere
Aly tilts the scales.

Moving closer upon the fighters
he bends down towards them
and shouts the impending doom,
"He who dishonors his ancestors
curses himself!"

And without even a second thought
all of us. including me, join in—
"Curses himself!
Curses himself!
Curses himself!

And at that
Not-with-us
loses his will to fight.

Within moments,
the bloodied Crocodile,
crawls triumphantly from beneath him
holding to keys to our chains.

He unfastens Suma from our line
and leads him to another line
directly in front of us.
Suma smiles a bit
at my nod of respect
then openly declares,
    "Look Queen Ramatoulaye,
    in the distance, the land!"

...the land, I whisper, the land...

the simple words
echoing and swelling
all around me
in low, mournful cries.

I turn to my people
and open my mouth to speak.

Our fight on that toubob land
will be a most bitter one, my people!
There will, no doubt, be more rapes,
more violations, more beatings,
more sickness, diseases, and more horrors.
But just as Suma,
outwitted the toubob here on this boat
and moved from one line to another
you must find a way to defy the death

intended for you in this place—
It is not enough that on this boat

you have had to swallow your own tears,
and drink your own blood!
Now, you must carve
through the bile and guts and evil of this place
for your own deliverance!
But remember, my people, remember!
Remember, no matter what,
that you are still Anansi's children—Ashe,
and you are still the Creator's own!

"Ashe" they whisper back to me,
"Ashe," they say again
until the chains are almost silent.

We stand starring
at the land in the distance.

Then suddenly the toubob begin
rushing us with water—
They even give us soap.
We work it into our hair,
under our arms,
as in a dream,
all over our bodies.

We watch as the dark suds
fall to the floor.
The toubob pass out
small strips of cloth
that we fasten over our nakedness.

In time the boat is anchored
and there are toubob faces everywhere.

And in time again
we begin to move from the boat.

We step
 and we step
until we finally feel
the dark familiarity
of our mother again.

Great God of our striving souls—
Be ever with us in the place!

And while the toubob busy themselves
over papers and greetings
I look across at Suma
and embrace him with my spirit.
I look at Aly, and Fanta, and Bamidele,
and all those countless others

who will have to continue bravely
this awesome struggle
that we have only begun—

But you can't chain the spirit!
Oh no, you can't chain the sun!

Illustration: You Can't Chain the Spirit!